Contents

What are screws?

A screw has a **groove** which winds round and round. The groove is a spiral shape. It is called a **thread**. When you turn a wood screw the thread cuts into the wood.

With each turn the screw is pulled into the wood by one thickness of the thread. After several turns the screw is firmly in place.

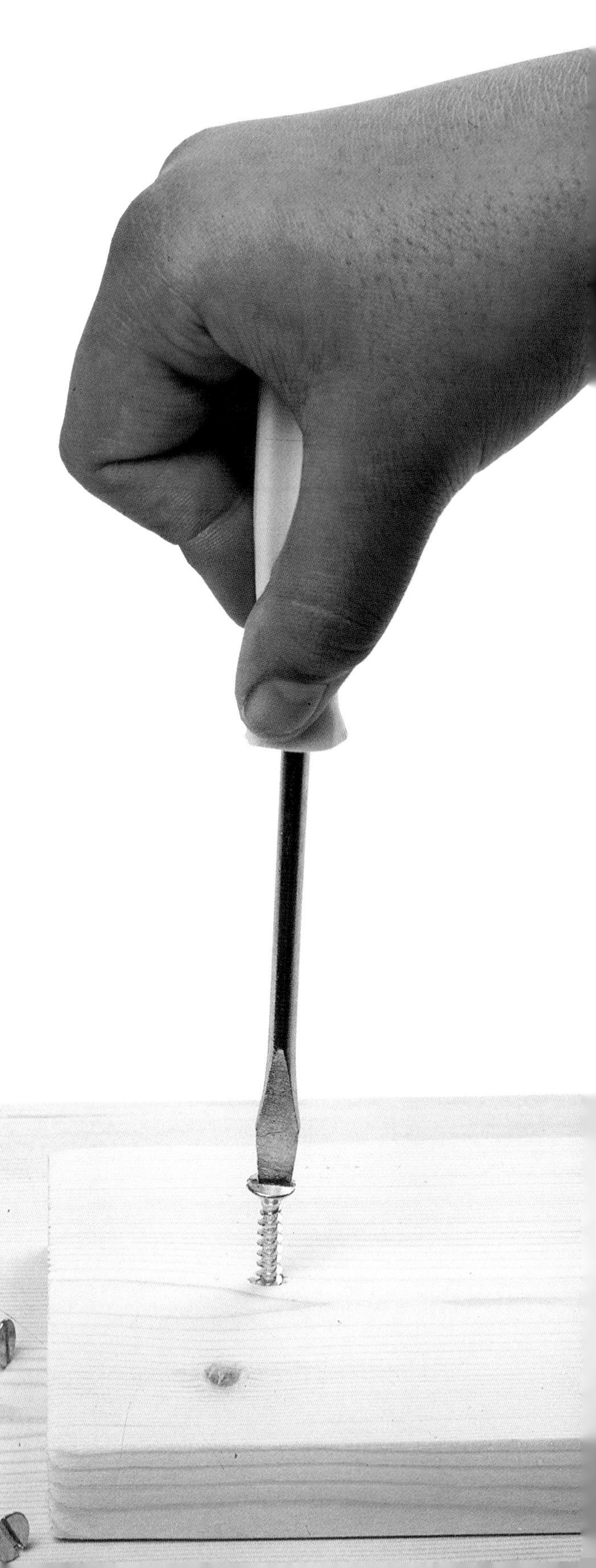

what d
Screws
do?

David Glover

First published in Great Britain by Heinemann Library
Halley Court, Jordan Hill, Oxford OX2 8EJ
a division of Reed Educational & Professional Publishing Ltd.

MELBOURNE AUCKLAND
FLORENCE PRAGUE MADRID ATHENS
SINGAPORE TOKYO SÃO PAULO
CHICAGO PORTSMOUTH NH MEXICO
IBADAN GABORONE JOHANNESBURG
KAMPALA NAIROBI

Designed by Celia Floyd and Sharon Rudd
Illustrated by Barry Atkinson (pp5, 15, 17, 18, 23) and Douglas Hall (p11)
Printed in Hong Kong / China

00 99 98
10 9 8 7 6 5 4 3 2

ISBN 0 431 06263 3
This title is also available in a hardback library edition (ISBN 0 431 06262 5).

British Library Cataloguing in Publication Data
Glover, David
What do screws do?
1. Screws – Juvenile literature
I. Title II. Screws
621.8'82

Acknowledgements
The Publishers would like to thank the following for permission to reproduce photographs:
Trevor Clifford pp4, 6, 7, 8, 9, 10, 11, 14, 18, 20, 21; Robert Harding Picture Library p12;
Zefa pp13, 17; Trip/J Ringland p15; Spectrum Colour Library p22.

Cover photograph by Trevor Clifford
Commissioned photography arranged by Hilary Fletcher
Special thanks to Jack, Bejal and Rose who appear in the photographs.

Thanks to David Byrne for his comments on the initial draft.

The Publishers would like to thank Toys R Us Ltd The Worlds Biggest Toy Megastore, NES Arnold Ltd, Do It All Ltd and Halfords for the kind loan of equipment and material used in this book.

Every effort has been made to contact copyright holders of any material reproduced in this book. Any omissions will be rectified in subsequent printings if notice is given to the Publisher.

You could not push a screw into wood with your bare hands. The screw thread **magnifies** your strength by winding the screw in a little at a time.

With screw threads you can tighten and grip things. You can do this with much more force than you can by pushing or pulling.

FACT

Screw strength

Screws magnify your strength. All your effort to turn them is concentrated into small movements inwards.

FILE

Lids and caps

This lemonade bottle has a screw cap. The top holds on tightly enough to stop the gas from escaping. You must remember to screw the cap back on tightly after you have poured a drink.

When you screw down the cap it squashes a small circle of card or plastic onto the neck of the bottle. This makes a tight **seal** that keeps in the gas.

Screw caps on jars help to keep food fresh. They seal tightly enough to stop **germs** getting in to the jar. They also stop the food inside from drying out.

FACT

Popping corks

Some fizzy drinks are stored in bottles with corks. The cork has to be held on with wire to stop it from popping out. These bottles are difficult to seal once they have been opened.

Nuts and bolts

Nuts and **bolts** hold things together. The **thread** on a bolt screws into the thread inside a nut.

You can use a **spanner** to tighten a nut. With a spanner you can make a nut so tight that it will hold the wheels on your bike. Nuts will even hold the engine in place inside a car.

Nuts have different shapes. Some have wings so that you can turn them with your fingers. Some nuts are square. The most common shape is a hexagonal nut with six sides.

FACT FILE

Spanner power!

You can make a nut tighter with a spanner than you can with your fingers. A long spanner helps you tighten with more power than a short one.

Corkscrews and drills

As you turn a corkscrew it winds slowly into the cork. The corkscrew grips the cork tightly enough for you to pull the cork out of the bottle.

Sharp edges on the end of a drillbit cut into the wood. The drillbit has a spiral thread. The **thread** winds the waste wood back from the hole.

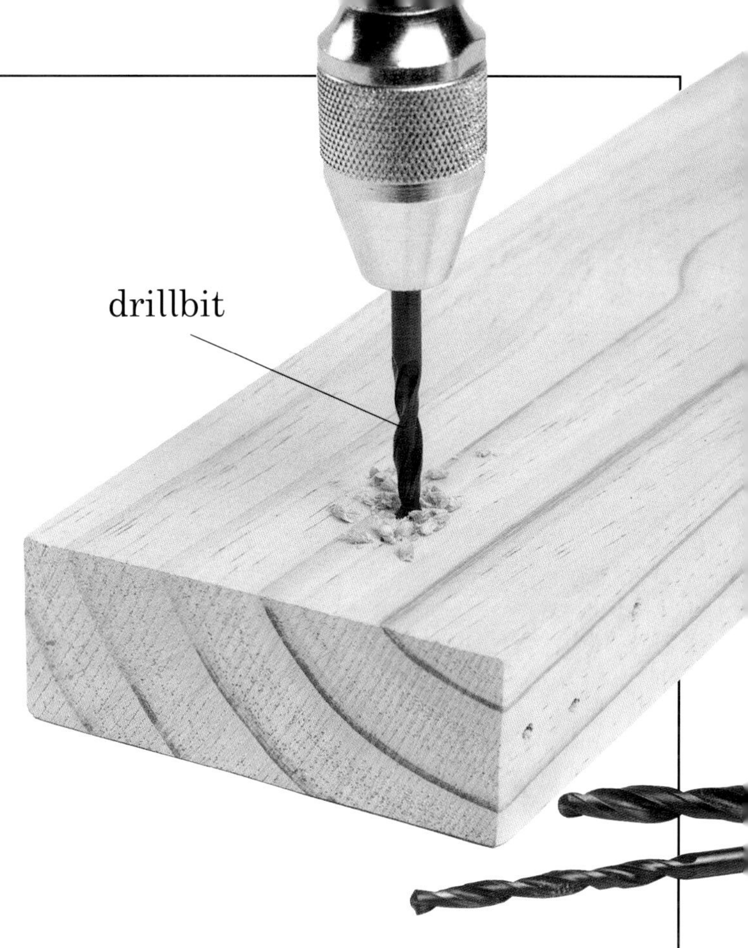

An **auger** is a very large drill. It is used to make big holes, for example to plant fence posts or trees. The auger has a wide screw thread. The thread winds the soil out of the hole.

FACT

Small and big holes

You use more effort to turn a large drill than a small one. You can make a small hole in wood with a hand drill. You need a large power drill to make a big hole in metal or concrete.

FILE

Staircases and slides

A spiral staircase is like a giant screw that you climb. You move up higher each time you go around the staircase. The spiral spreads the climbing over a longer distance. This means that each upward step takes less effort than when you climb straight up.

A spiral slide is great fun! Gravity (the force that makes things fall) pulls you down the slide. The spiral spins you around. A helter-skelter is a spiral fairground slide. Some water chutes use the same idea.

FACT

Which way round?

Spiral staircases nearly always go up clockwise. This means that as you go up you turn in the same direction as the hands on a clock. Most people find it easier to come down a spiral staircase, when they move round anticlockwise.

FILE

Tops and props

This spinning top is turned by a screw **thread**. When you push the knob down, the thread makes the top spin.

The **propellers** on aeroplanes are sometimes called props or air screws. The **blades** are twisted so that they pull the plane through the air as they turn. They screw through the air like a wood screw pushing into wood.

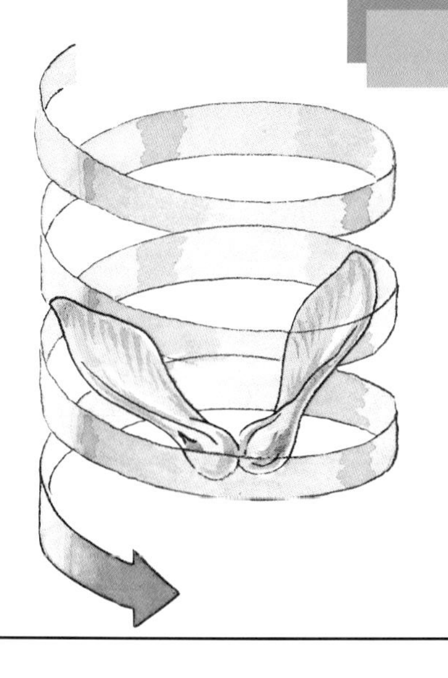

FACT

Sycamore spinners

The seeds of sycamore trees have wings like propellers. They spin round as they fall.

FILE

Water screws

An Archimedes screw is a kind of **water pump**. It moves water from one place to another. The turning screw winds water up from a lower level to a higher one.

FACT

Ancient screws

Archimedes was a scientist in ancient Greece. He invented the Archimedes screw more than 2000 years ago. It is a kind of pump that farmers in some countries still use today.

FILE

The propeller on this boat is a water screw. As the blades spin they push water backwards. This pushes the boat forwards in the same way as gas rushing backwards from a rocket or a jet engine.

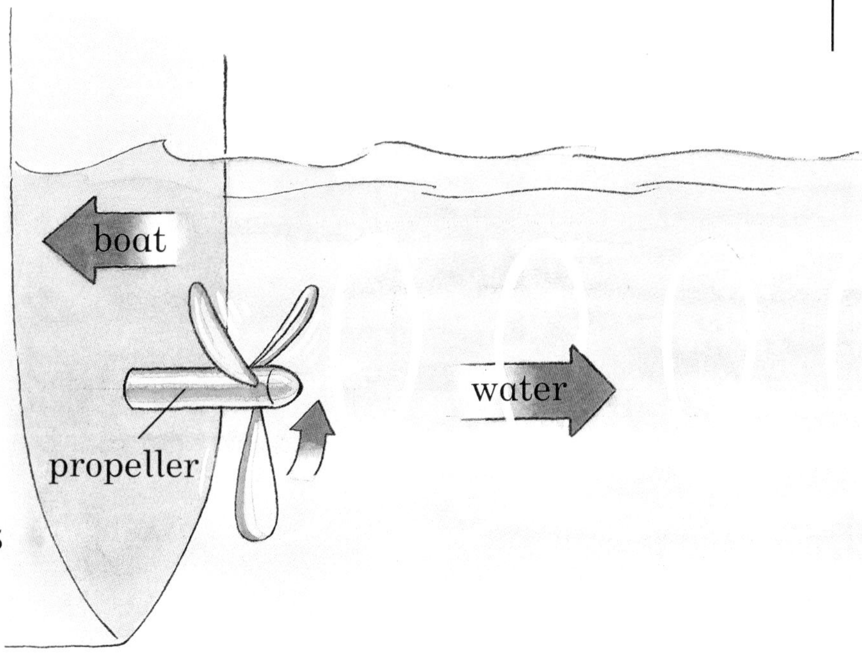

Hoses and taps

Lengths of garden hose are joined together with screw joints. The screw **threads** hold the pieces together tightly so that no water leaks out.

The water for the hose is turned on and off with a tap.

The screw inside the tap **magnifies** the force from your fingers as you turn the tap. The screw moves a rubber washer up or down. The washer blocks or unblocks a hole through which the water flows.

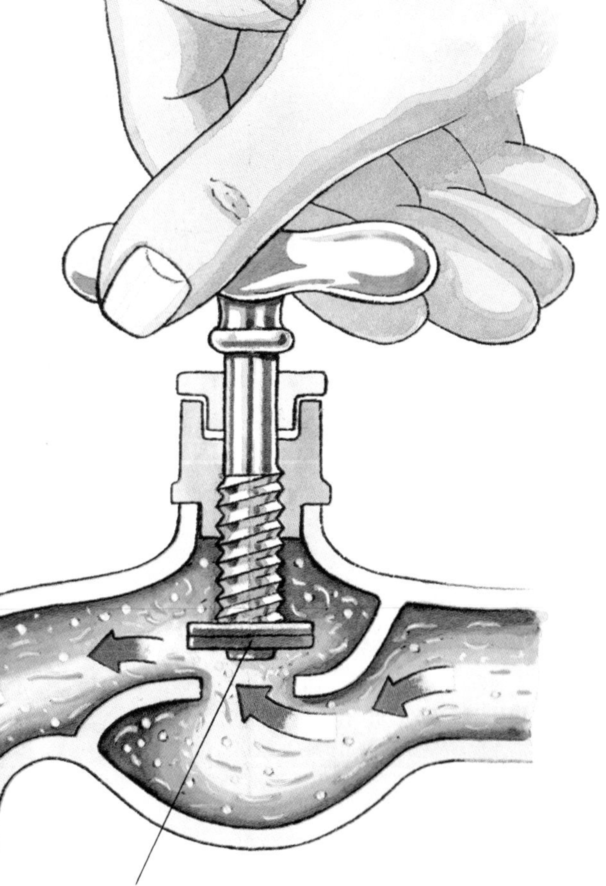

FACT

Squirting water

The force of the water inside a tap can be powerful. Turn on a garden hose and try to stop the water with your thumb. It squirts out everywhere!

FILE

Jacks and clamps

Can a small person lift a car with their bare hands? That person can using a **screw jack**. When the screw is turned, this **magnifies** the strength in the person's arms. The car rises a little at a time.

Warning: Screw jacks should only be used by adults. Lifting cars can be very dangerous.

A workshop **vice** holds things firmly for sawing, bending and hammering. A screw moves the jaws of the vice.

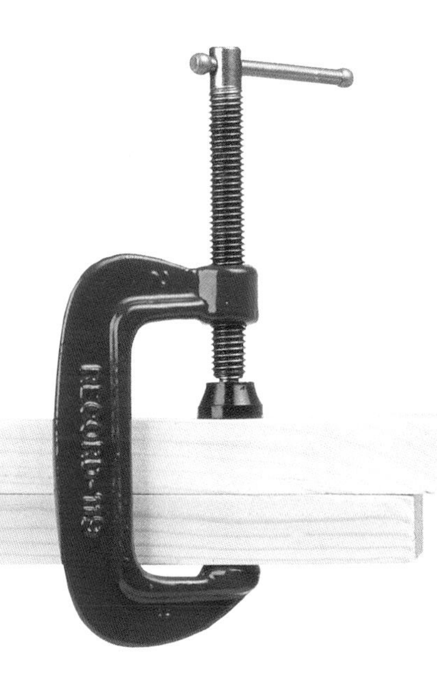

A **G-clamp** holds parts together while the glue dries. G-clamps come in many sizes, from tiny ones to huge ones!

Tunnel borers

How do you dig a tunnel under the sea-bed? You dig it with a machine that cuts through the rock like a giant drill.

Tunnel-boring machines are like giant drills. They have spinning **blades** at the front. As the machine is pushed forwards, the blades cut into the rock. The cut rock passes back through holes in the blades. It is taken out of the tunnel by train.

The Channel Tunnel goes under the sea between England and France. Eleven huge tunnel-boring machines took six years to build it.

FACT

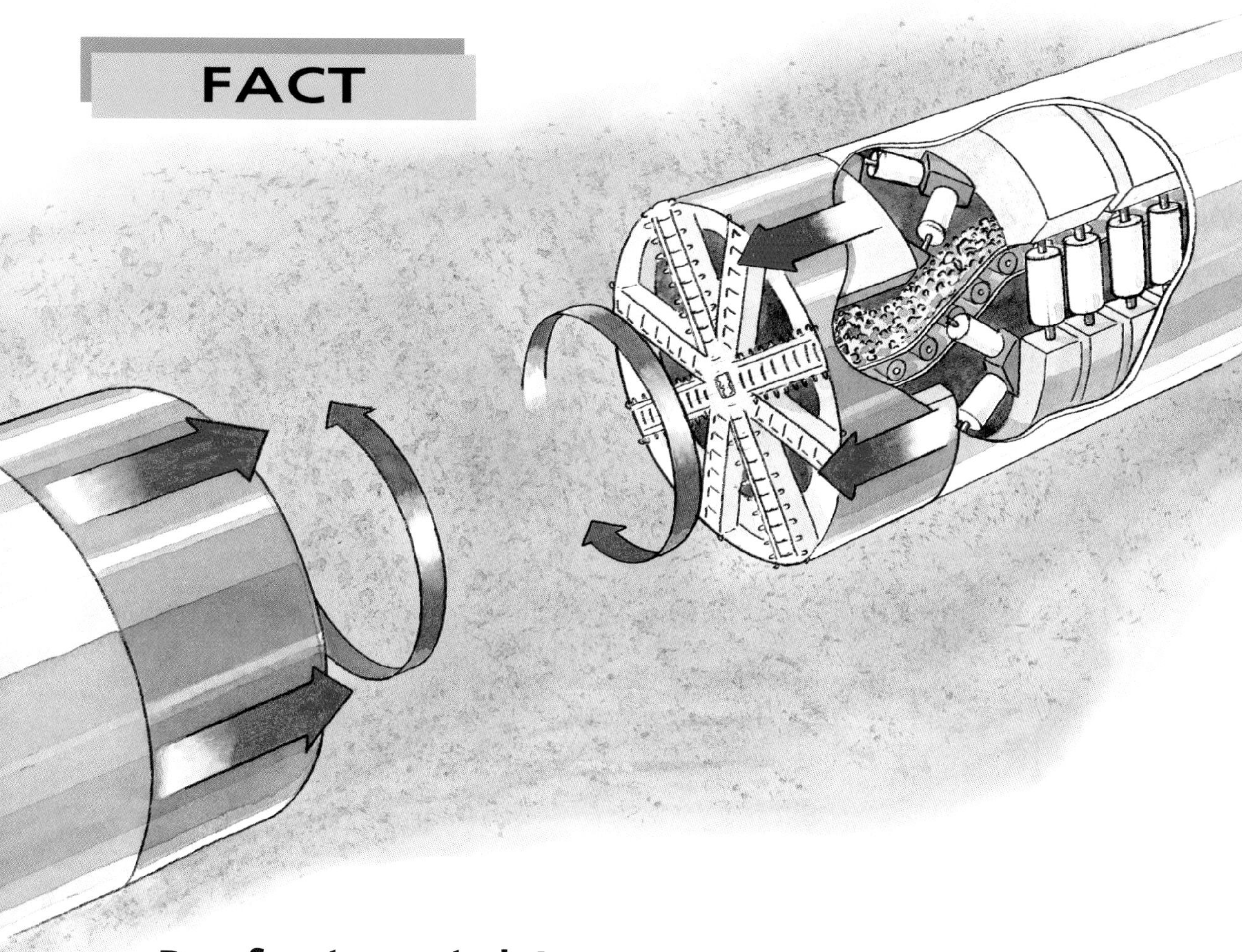

Perfect match!

Machines started the Channel Tunnel from both ends at the same time. The machines moved forwards about one metre each hour. The two halves of the tunnel lined up perfectly when the machines met in the middle.

FILE

Glossary

auger A tool for drilling large holes.

blade The sharp cutting part of a knife.

bolt A type of screw used with a nut, for holding things together.

germs Micro-organisms which can cause disease.

grooves Long narrow channels, cut into something.

magnify To make bigger.

nut Something which screws onto the end of a bolt to hold things together.

propellers Blades which spin round to pull a plane through the air or push a boat through water.

seal To close something very tightly.

screw jack A machine used for raising heavy objects.

spanner A tool used for turning a nut.

thread The spiral groove around a bolt or screw.

vice An instrument with jaws used for holding things steady.

water pump A machine for raising water up from deep in the ground.

Index